Nearer to God

How to Pray with Prophetic Power

by
Ken and Tracy Lee Karner

Rose Hall Media Company
St. Cloud, Minnesota
rosehallmedia.com

Library of Congress cataloging-in-publication data:

Karner, Ken
Karner, Tracy Lee
Nearer to God: How to Pray with Prophetic Power / Ken and Tracy Lee Karner
cm
ISBN 978-0-9655922-5-3

1. Christianity—Prayer 2. Bible—Devotional Use. 3. The Psalms—Contemporary Translation

Published by Rose Hall Media Company, St. Cloud, Minnesota

rosehallmedia.com

Rose Hall
Media
Company

for our children

Contents

Pray with prophetic power, beginning today

If today you hear His voice, do not harden your hearts.[1]

Look around.

Earthquakes, hurricanes, tsunamis. Suicide bombers. Mass extinction of species. Bankruptcies and foreclosures. Stalkers, rapists and murderers. Fat cats take $60-million-plus annual salaries while millions of people go without healthcare. Impoverished third-world citizens work in appallingly dangerous conditions just to subsist. And those who have dedicated themselves to serving their "company" for decades, lose their pensions. The young rebel and the old despair.

Neighbors don't know their neighbors' names. Members of families disown each other. People mask their loneliness and alienation under addiction, materialism and thrill-seeking, or they sink into the pit of despair.

God is calling us to pray.

Look within.

Our hearts are anxious and restless. We experience pain caused by our own and our fellow humans' selfishness, greed,

---

1   Hebrews 3:15

betrayal, and anger. How do we respond to hopelessness and disillusionment, resentment and bitterness? How do we put an end to lies, hatred, addictions, vindictive blame, self-aggrandizement and self-loathing? How do we fulfill our hearts' desire for peace, healing, reconciliation, restoration and renewal?

God is calling us to pray.

When we want to be set free from anxiety and fear, when we long for the freedom that comes from knowing truth, when our souls thirst for God's perfect justice and long to experience His loving kindness, then we draw nearer to God in prayer.

Powerful prayer is not merely a path to inner tranquility. Prayer unites us to God's purpose, and enables us to facilitate peace, love and justice in this hurting world. Prayer brings hope, into maddening, frightening, overwhelming and seemingly impossible situations.

Although this book sets up one "formula" as a way to quiet our hearts and enter into the presence of God, powerful prayer is not a formulaic ritual for us to master. Powerful prayer isn't really about us at all.

Powerful prayer teaches us to recognize, trust and glorify God's power.

This is a journey made of daily steps, taking us ever deeper into the truth of who God is, what God can do, who we are to God, how God wants us to live, and the immeasurable grace of the help God offers to us. In other words, powerful prayer is a relationship. As with all relationships, there are things we can do to grow and strengthen that relationship, and things we can do to weaken and destroy it. This is a practical, not a theoretical prayer book. It is designed to help us be in relationship with God through prayer.

So, let us now begin our lifelong journey nearer to God.

Part One: Daily Prayer

1) A Map for the Journey

Jesus has promised us, his followers, that whatever we ask in his name, he will do.[1]

But what does it mean, to pray in Jesus' name? For what should we (and for what should we *not*) ask?

What should we pray and how can we pray effectively, so that our prayers will release the power of God to accomplish great things in our lives?

To pray with prophetic power is to believe the word of God and speak it, in the name of Jesus Christ[2] by the power of the Holy Spirit,[3] into our particular, situations, triumphs, problems, joys and concerns[4].

To do this, we must draw nearer to God. We give ourselves to God, in love, so that we may live according to God's purpose and plan. This book is like a map for drawing nearer to God, so that we can know and do his will.

Effective prayer is union with God. When we pray, we journey into a deeper, more loving relationship with God. Effective prayer is the decision to *move*, deliberately and

---

1   John 14:13-14
2   Colossians 3:17
3   1 Corinthians 14:14-15
4   Philippians 4:6

repeatedly, *nearer to God*. Every single day, we must *go* in the right direction. Here's how:

- We spend time with God in prayer and scripture study;

- and we make spending time with God our highest priority.

We find God in His Word

Remember, this book is only a map. Please do not mistake the map for the journey. To get where we want to go, we can't merely read *about* the journey; we have to personally *take* the journey. The journey is a lifelong commitment to *prayer and study.*

Every principle in this book is taken from the Bible, but we do not extensively quote the Bible. We give references, so that you can open your Bible and read for yourself. Look up every single footnote we reference, and read the verses in context.

To walk daily toward God, we must hear and ponder his word, then we must do what his word tells us to do. We bury God's word in our own hearts like a treasure, to keep it safely stored there.[5]

We make God our Priority

Our daily habits indicate what we value, what matters most to us.

Every minute of every day, we make decisions. And each decision is a move—toward or away from God.

---

5   Psalm 119:11

When we love God, we make God our priority. We spend time alone with God. We turn off the distractions – put away the cell phone; turn off the television and radio; refuse to be interrupted. We retreat to a private room and close the door and spend *time alone with God*, in prayer and in reading scripture, in an appropriately reverent, private place, *every day*.

Set aside ten to fifteen minutes daily for private prayer, and another ten to fifteen minutes for scripture study. If you can't make time right now, look at your schedule and make time later today. If you can't do it today, then figure out a way to do it this week, and then strive for 2-3 times per week, gradually incorporating this daily prayer and spiritual reading into your daily life.

If we can't make time for private prayer, if we won't study what God's word says about prayer, then our habits and our lifestyle have made it clear that our hearts, our minds, our souls and our strength belong not to God, but instead to the material world.

And when we consistently allow the busy world to lure us away from our necessary time alone with God, then we must consider what our actions say about our values. Is friendship with the world more important to us than being God's children?[6]

Let us choose to make God our first priority, and let us begin, today, to draw nearer to God.

---

6   James 4:4

2) The Prayers

We have already stated that prayer is a journey. We do not have to be expert travelers in order to begin the journey. We simply start from where we are. This guidance from the book of James in the Bible places us firmly on the right path.

Lessons from James

James, in his letter to 1st Century believers, says that some prayers are effective, while others are not.[1] He also explains exactly what we must do in order to draw near to God, so that God will hear our prayers. He tells us to:

- submit to God;
- resist the devil;
- draw near to God;
- cleanse our hands;
- purify our hearts;
- and repent.[2]

Following these instructions for drawing near to God, assures us that God will meet us and hear us.

---

1   James 4:3
2   James 4:7-11

The Holy Spirit is our Teacher

The lust to discover new ideas and new technologies, to join the latest fads and follow the most popular gurus is not spiritual; it's worldly. Nothing and no one can show us the way to God as clearly and precisely as the Holy Spirit, who speaks to us through the ancient, Spirit-inspired words of the Bible.[1]

In universities, governments and businesses, promotions and higher salaries usually go to those who spout complicated ideas loaded with pretentious professional jargon. But God's word admonishes us to beware of anything that would complicate the purity and simplicity of devotion to Jesus Christ. Therefore we recommend simple, timeless forms of` prayer as the best way, every day.

4 Traditional Prayers

We use four traditional prayers, which help us to follow James' instructions for approaching God. Praying these four prayers every day prepares us for a deeper communion with God. These prayers lead us away from our present concerns and preoccupations, where our scattered and distracted thoughts prevent us from listening to God. They serve as a transition into a quietly meditative state of mind, in which we can hear God.

The Jesus Prayer

God does not permit us to enter into his holy presence when we are filthy with sin. But because he loves us, he has provided for our cleansing.

---

1 1st John 2:27

Whenever we acknowledge that we are sinners, confessing that only the blood of Jesus can wash away our guilt, we take the first step of our spiritual journey home to heaven, which is also the first step of our daily journey nearer to God.[2]

The words of the Jesus Prayer are:

Lord Jesus Christ, Son of God, have mercy on me, a sinner.

The Jesus Prayer is based on the tax collector's prayer, found in the Gospel of Luke. Jesus said that this simple, humble prayer justifies (cleanses) the one who prays.[3]

Jesus tells the story of two very different prayers, prayed by two very different men. He contrasts the words and attitude of the tax collector (the penitent sinner who asks for mercy) with the words and demeanor of a Pharisee (a piously religious man).

The pious man, the Pharisee, thanks God that he is better than other people. He sees himself as superior to "sinners." To him, sinners are those who cheat, who are unjust, who commit adultery. The Pharissee knows that the tax collector, who uses his position for his own enrichment, is a sinner. Comparing himself to other sinners, the Pharissee assumes he is not one of them. So he lists his own virtues: he fasts twice a week; and he tithes.

Not only does the Pharisee's piety fail to cleanse him, but God clearly disapproves of this manner and method of prayer.[4] He turns away from those who pray like this.

In the act of confessing our sinful natures, we are cleansed.[5] And so we begin with the tax collector's prayer, of which God approves.

---

2   1st John 1:7
3   Luke 18:14
4   Luke 18:9-14
5   1st John 1:9

When we pray this prayer penitently and honestly, we can be confident that we may enter into the presence of our heavenly Father and present our requests to him.

The Strength Prayer

The forces of evil, the powers of the world and the impulses of our selfish instincts are too great for us to overcome by our own strength.[6] But we are not alone. God, in his graciousness, provides the strength we need.[7] We simply have to admit our weakness and ask for God's help.[8] The words of the strength prayer are:

Lord grant me the strength to resist the devil, the world, and my own sinful nature.

King David's Prayer

King David's prayer has been used by Jews and Christians for millennia. When we pray these words with conviction and integrity, we train our minds to decisively reject impure, selfish, hateful, greedy, lustful or any other ungodly thoughts or words. This prepares our hearts to be purely devoted to God, in order that God's Spirit may dwell within us.

The words of King David's Prayer are:

May the words of my mouth and even my innermost thoughts be acceptable to you, O Lord, my Strength, and my Redeemer.

---

6   Ephesians 6:12
7   Psalm 28:7
8   Isaiah 40:29

The Lord's Prayer

The Lord's Prayer very specifically asks God to be present in our lives here on earth, to satisfy our basic needs and to protect us from the powers of evil, which are stronger than we are. By instructing us to "pray in this manner," Jesus is showing us what we are supposed to pray for and about.

We approach God confidently, as his beloved children, conscious that, as members of the holy, universal church, it is our duty to build strength and unity in the family of Christ.

Our dear, heavenly Father

We are assured that as a loving Father, God cares about the needs and desires of all of his children. Therefore it is proper for us to call on him with the words, *"Our Father, who art in heaven."*

Honored be Your holy name

God's name is holy, and we are to honor it. When we speak the words, *"Hallowed be Thy name,"* we repent of spiritual irreverence and apathy. We forsake all unholy actions and thoughts by which we profane the name of God or fail to present ourselves to the world as His holy children.

May Your kingdom come soon

In saying, *"Thy kingdom come,"* we seek to understand that God's kingdom dwells within us, and we are called to demonstrate this to the world. We also recognize that when His physical kingdom comes, all sin will be abolished on earth.

May Your will be done on earth as it is in Heaven

God does not need our prayers to accomplish His will. But we pray for ourselves and for others, that God will give each of us the knowledge, the courage, and the fortitude to obey His will.

When we pray, *"Thy will be done on earth as it is in heaven,"* we repent of prideful, resentful, violent, and rebellious thoughts. We repent for lusting after the enticements of the world. We repent for believing that we are rightly entitled to more than we've been given. We ask God to break the powers that trap us in self-absorption, that we may be free, by God's grace and with his help, to know and do his will.

Bless us each day with our daily bread

Even without our prayers, God provides food, drink, clothing, shelter and supplies, civil order, family, friends, and community—even for those who oppose him. When we pray, *"Give us this day our daily bread,"* we are asking him to help us understand the breadth and depth of his provision, that we may receive our many gifts with thanksgiving.

With this words we also repent of dissatisfaction and anxiety, and ask God to instill a grateful spirit in us. We ask that he strengthen our faith so we will fully trust in his divine providence, knowing he will supply, in due time, our necessary shelter, nourishment, protection and peace.

Forgive our sins as we forgive those who sin against us

With these words, we recognize that we sin daily—many times—and therefore are unworthy and undeserving of the things for which we pray. We humbly ask God to have mercy, to count our faith as righteousness, and by his abundant grace grant our requests. We also acknowledge that we must therefore heartily and readily forgive those who have sinned against us.

Lead us away from temptation

God tempts no one. We recognize that the devil, the world, and our own flesh deceive and seduce us into unbelief, despair, corruption, immorality, perversion and depravity. With the words, *"Lead us not into tempation,"* we ask God to guard us, protect us, and give us the strength to overcome temptations, that we may remain victoriously obedient to his word.

We also repent of the prideful notion that we are too strong to be deceived or seduced by temptation. We ask God to lead us away from the places and situations that would tempt us, and also to give us the power to resist temptation. We request: wisdom to recognize the devil's pervasive lies; strength to resist the world's allures; and discipline to overcome our selfish instincts.

Please, Father, deliver us from all evil

We acknowledge that in this world evil and corruption exist. We are defenceless against their power to harm us body and soul. We therefore ask God to deliver us from every form of evil, praying, *"Deliver us from evil."*

In Jesus' name, Amen.

Jesus himself taught us to pray in this manner, therefore we are confident that this prayer is acceptable to our heavenly Father. *Amen* means *yes, it is true.*[9]

---

9 Many ideas in this section are from the writings of Martin Luther, the 16th Century church reformer who was opposed to uttering prayers in the manner of magical incantations, and taught his followers to pray mindfully, from the heart..

The Psalms

It is God's will that we delight in his law and continually and joyfully contemplate his precepts. Praying Psalms—the ageless prayers given to us by the Holy Spirit—helps us relinquish our prideful ambitions and submit our thoughts, decisions and actions to the word of God.

Psalms help us pray the word of God into our present situations and over all the problems that concern us, allowing the counsel of the Holy Spirit to guide us.

When praying in this manner, we will often find ourselves speaking in the present tense while praying about a future truth. For example, when we say, "Oh, how I love your law; all day long I contemplate your precepts," our words may not yet feel accurate. In faith, we recognize that when we prayerfully enter into the presence of God, our future sanctification and salvation become presently real.

As we daily pray Psalms, we open our hearts and engage our minds. In faith, we understand that the Holy Spirit will teach us everything we need to know, as long as we keep putting into practice what we have learned. We strive to listen to the word of God and *obey* it.

Even when we pray privately, we are not praying Psalms alone. Every day, at all hours, Psalms are being prayed by members of the universal Christian church.

When we pray Psalms, we join our voices to the chorus of the communion of saints.

When we approach Psalms looking for an answer to a problem, or to express a need or feeling, we most often are thinking of ourselves or people to whom we feel close. The word of God enlarges our capacity to humble ourselves and to pray for others, even for those we do not personally know. We will often find an emotion or situation in a psalm that feels contrary to our present mood or circumstance. In those instances, we let the words of God enlighten us to the situations and needs of our brothers and sisters around the world, because we are called to bear each other's joys and sorrows. And sometimes, Psalms reveal hidden truths of our own hearts—the anger, fear, or hurt, which we may be attempting to cover up or deny.

Psalms are as complex and difficult as the human heart, full of seemingly contradictory emotion.

These ancient prayers show us that God knows everything about our thoughts and desires, even the ideas and wishes we may not want to acknowledge.

Psalms are as paradoxical as life.

They are at once individual and communal. In them, within the circumstances of our ordinary, daily lives, we encounter the holiness of God. And through them, the inevitable pain of living on earth is simultaneously expressed and transcended.

Above all, **Psalms teach us the important spiritual discipline of restfully *waiting* for the Lord to speak** in our hearts, to reveal His will, and to act.

Developing the habit of praying Psalms each day, no matter what our mood or situation, is a practice which deeply transforms us, molding us into bondservants who love our Master, who desire nothing more than to be near God, that we may know and do God's will.

3) Preparing for Prophetically Powerful Prayer

In order to achieve prophetically powerful prayer, we must first assess our compliance with eight biblical ordinances. It is useful to slowly ponder the list on the following page, asking ourselves if we are prepared to enter into the presence of our Holy, Almighty God.

If we find we are noncompliant with any item on this list, we should stop and remedy the problem before proceeding to pray, otherwise, we cannot expect God to draw near to us and hear us.

It is also helpful to frequently review this list.

(Now turn the page and ponder the ordinances.)

- Ask in faith, without doubt.[1]

- Be humble.[2]

- Repent; confess your sins.[3]

- Do not pray mindlessly, or babble endless words.[4]

- Do not expect God to magically grant your wishes when your life is offensive to God: when you are participating in evil activities; when you are failing to do good deeds; when you are apathetic about injustice instead of fighting for justice; when you fail to speak out against those who take advantage of poor, weak or defenseless people. Your prayers, when you are not actively living *for* God, might be an abomination to God.[5] Instead of demanding your own way, acknowledge the truth about your life, and ask God to help you change your ways.

- Do not pray if you harbor unforgiveness in your heart.[6]

- Do not pray for personal gain.[7]

- Pray without ceasing; strive to pray daily, and often throughout the day.[8]

- Pray in Jesus' name.[9]

(When your heart is right and you are prepared to enter into the presence of God, continue by reading the next page.)

1	James 1:6
2	James 4:6
3	Psalm 32:5-6
4	Matthew 6:7
5	Isaiah 1:11-17
6	Mark 11:25
7	James 4:3
8	1st Thessalonians 5:17
9	John 14:13

Prophetically powerful prayer is heartfelt, personal prayer. Certainly there is a place for public and communal prayer, but when you pray in public, be certaain you are not praying in a self-congratulatory manner, to show off or to draw attention to your piety, your eloquence or your knowledge. That's what the Pharisee did.[1]

When seeking to pray with prophetic power, it is important to find time to pray alone, apart from even our closest family and friends, like Jesus did in the garden of Gethsemene.2 While it is important to also pray communically, we need to learn to do this in the most humble of manners, joining into the prayers of our community without drawing attention to ourselves.

Private and communal prayer are both important to our spiritual growth, and neither should replace the other. This book however, does not address how to pray communally. This is about our private prayer lives, training our hearts to seek and listen to God.

After you have prepared your heart to pray and removed yourself to a quiet, private place, transition into a meditative state of mind.

Read a prayer slowly, then close your eyes and repeat it from memory, once, or perhaps twice as the Holy Spirit moves you to understand the deep meaning of the words. Do this with each of the four ancient prayers, making sure that you are not uttering them mindlessly. Think about the words and intentionally mean them.

(Now turn to page 24 and pray.)

---

1   Matthew 6:5-6
2   Mark 14:32-41

4) A Formula for Prophetically Powerful Prayer

Lord Jesus Christ,
Son of God,
have mercy on me,
a sinner.

Lord, grant me the strength
to resist the devil,
the world,
and my own sinful nature.

May the words of my mouth
and even my innermost thoughts
be acceptable to you, O Lord,
my Strength,
and my Redeemer.

Our Father, who art in heaven,
Hallowed by Thy name.
Thy kingdom come.
Thy will be done on earth as it is in heaven;
Give us this day our daily bread;
And forgive us our trespasses, as we forgive
those who trespass against us.
Lead us not into temptation,
and deliver us from evil.
In Jesus' name, Amen.

(Now turn the page.)

The Psalms

Scan pages 27-29 to select a prayer corresponding to a celebration, desire, emotion, need or trial, which you are experiencing today. Turn to that page and pray the Psalm.

Personal Prayer

After praying the Psalm of the day, offer your own personal prayers to God, with thanksgiving.[1]

Listen to God

Now use Part Two (page 124) of this book, the *Daily Scripture Study*, to intentionally and deeply listen to God.

Unceasing Prayer

All through the day, praise God and repent. Bring Him your concerns and needs--for yourself, your loved ones, your neighbors and your enemies--with thanksgiving. Seek to fill your mind with psalms, hymns and spiritual songs.[2] And any time the Spirit moves you, talk to God.

---

1   Philippians 4:6
2   Ephesians 5:19

Celebrations

Desires

Feelings

Needs

Trials

5) Psalms

The Psalms are ancient prayers, full of wisdom to enlighten our minds and open our hearts. This enables the Holy Spirit to convict and sanctify us, that we may be transformed into God's holy people.

When we pray a Psalm, we read slowly, line by line, taking time to ponder the words' meaning. As we do this, we begin to understand what it means to pray "in the Spirit."[1]

**The prayers on the following pages
are our own contemporary translations
of the ancient Hebrew Psalms.**

---

1   Ephesians 6:18

A Prayer to Celebrate Release

Hallelujah, praise the Lord.

It is good to sing praises to our God;

it makes us joyful to extol his name.

The Lord rebuilds our hope after devastation.

He returns the captives—the prisoners of war—to their homeland.

He heals the broken hearted; he dresses their wounds.

He has numbered each star and given each one its name.

How great is the Lord; how powerful his strength.

His wisdom is immeasurable.

The Lord lifts up the downtrodden and crushes their oppressors into the dust.

Sing songs of thanksgiving to the Lord.

Play the harp for our God.

He covers the heavens with clouds that produce rain.

He makes the prairies and meadows to thrive;

He gives food to the animals, even to the ravens when they squawk with hunger.

Nearly everyone believes that large armies can protect them.

But God is not impressed by, nor does he need, an arsenal of weapons and bombs.

He finds pleasure in those who honor Him;

Psalm 147

He grants favor to those who expectantly wait for his salvation.

All you his people, praise the Lord.

All you who dwell in the city of God, praise your God!

He provides protection within your fortress walls; he blesses your children.

He gives peace and prosperity to Your country; at every harvest he provides bountiful yields.

Our powerful God uttered a word and the earth was formed,

by His command He created the universe.

He makes it to snow in dense flakes; he covers the earth in frost.

His hailstones pelt the earth; he sends bone-chilling, unbearable cold.

When he commands it, the snow melts.

He causes the spring winds to blow and ice to thaw.

He has pronounced his word to Israel, to live according to his precepts and ordinances.

God has dealt uniquely with his chosen people; he has entrusted no other nation to be the priestly upholders of his law.

Hallelujah.

Psalm 147

A Prayer to Celebrate Renewal of Hope

Hallelujah, praise the Lord!
Praise the Lord of heaven:
praise him in the highest heights;
praise him, all His angels;
praise him you heavenly hosts;
praise him sun and moon;
praise him stars of light;
praise him in the farthest reaches of the universe;
praise him in the firmament beyond the heavens;

Let all creation praise the Lord!

By his command, everything was made.
He ordained each creature's place in the universe.
He gave each one natural laws to govern its existence.

Praise the Lord of earth:
  all whales, all creatures of the deep seas;
  lightning, hail, snow, fog, windy storm obeying the command of God;
  hills and mountains, fruit trees and conifers;
  wild and tame beasts, birds and worms;
  kings and citizens, rulers and leaders of the world;
  young men and women, old and young together;

Psalm 148

Everyone praise the Lord, for he alone is supreme.

His majesty extends over all the earth and all the universe;
He has renewed the strength and the hope of his people.
Therefore praise him, people of God;
you stood near to him and he remained faithful.

Hallelujah!

Psalm 148

A Prayer to Celebrate Renewal of Strength

I love the Lord!
He has heard my cry for help.
Indeed, he lowered Himself to listen to me;
I will turn to Him all the days of my life.

I felt imprisoned by Death's power;
fear of the grave overtook me.
I was completely despondent.
So I cried out to the Lord, I petitioned him,
"O my God, save me!"

How merciful is the Lord!
All that he promises, he fulfills.
Our God is full of compassion.
He protects all who are incapable of helping themselves.
I was in great danger
but the Lord rescued me from the grave.

So I remind myself, "Remain at peace--
the Lord has established your life to be good."
True--he rescued me from certain death.
He dried my tears and protected me from disaster.
I remain alive; near to him.
My faith in him remained unshaken

Psalm 116

even when I didn't know what to do,

even as I cried out in anguish,

when no one on earth could be trusted to help me.

How can I thank the Lord for all the goodness he has
shown to me?

At the thanksgiving meal, in front of everyone,

I will raise my glass, as a sign of my gratitude.

The Lord has rescued me--

I want everyone to know!

The Lord protects those who love him.

He values their love; he values their lives.

God, you are my Master;

I serve you as the saints served you.

You have torn me from Death's clutch;

therefore I bring you my pledge of obedience, with
thanksgiving.

I will proclaim loudly that you are my Lord.

In the presence of the people, in the court of your temple,

I will fulfill my holy vows to you.

Hallelujah.

Psalm 116

Thanksgiving for Comfort and Provision

Rejoice before the Lord, all people on earth!
Happily serve him;
come before him with joyful songs.

Recognize that the Lord is our God!
He made us to be his people;
we have not made ourselves.
He cares for us as a Shepherd cares for his flock.

Enter his temple gates with thanksgiving;
Enter the festival courtyard with loud applause.
Praise him! Extol him!
For the Lord is good to us.
His mercy endures forever;
He remains faithful to us for all eternity.

Psalm 100

Thanksgiving for Beauty and Bounty

Hallelujah, praise the Lord.

Praise him in His sanctuary!

Praise him, you powers of heaven!

Praise him for his mighty deeds!

Praise him for his immeasurable greatness!

Praise him with trumpets, with harps and zithers!

Praise him with tambourines and with dancing!

Praise him with sounding strings, with flutes and woodwinds!

Praise him with crashing cymbals and kettledrums!

Let all that lives—

let every breath and every movement of every creature—

be an endless song of praise to our God!

Psalm 150

Thanksgiving for God's Creation

The sky heralds God's grand majesty;

the vault of heaven testifies to the greatness of his creation.

One star narrates to the next and one night tells another;

they speak wordlessly, no one can hear their sounds.

Yet throughout all the earth we hear the language of creation;

its message reaches to the farthest countries.

God has pitched a tent in the sky for the sun.

In the morning it rises and radiates like a bridegroom at his wedding.

Certain of victory as a hero, the sun begins its course.

It grazes the horizon in its rising and its setting.

Nothing remains hidden from its heat.

The law of the Lord is perfect--it brings happiness.

You can depend on the commands of God.

If you have gone thoughtlessly about your daily life until now,

God's commands will make you wise.

God's arrangement of life's basic principles are steady and authoritative;

they delight the heart.

The instructions of God are clear;

the one who values them gains discernment and intelligent understanding.

Psalm 19

Reverence before God is good; awe will never cease.

The laws of the Lord are right, perfect and just;

   they are incomparably superior to gold,

   they are sweeter than the finest honey

Lord, I belong to you.

How good it is that your law warns me away from the
   wrong path!

Whoever keeps your commands will be richly rewarded.

But who can always recognize the right path?

Everyone veers off sometimes.

Please forgive me the sins I've committed without
   knowing,

   and protect me from conscienceless people.

Do not allow their prevailing power to control me.

With your guidance and protection I will be able to
   remain faithful to you;

   I want to be free from guilt, blameless.

Lord, let the words of my mouth and the thoughts of my
   mind please you.

In you I am secure--for you are my Savior!

Psalm 19

Thanksgiving for God's Eternal Sovereignty

Only the Lord is King!
  Grandeur cloaks him like a feast day vestment.
He is encircled by power.
He has laid the earth's foundations;
  his work does not falter nor crumble.

Lord, Your dominion is eternal;
  before time began, you already were.
The sea roars and clamors,
  the tides blare their mighty song;
  but even stronger than the thunder of violent waters,
  more powerful than a tsunami tidal surge
  is the Lord on high.

Lord, your word is true and trustworthy.
Your temple is the eternal dwelling place
of your holy presence.

Psalm 93

Thanksgiving for Guidance

L ord, you are so good to me,
  just as you have promised to be.

Please give me discernment and understanding because
  I trust in your word.

I went down many wrong paths before I finally admitted,
  I can't go on this way!

Therefore I now desire with all my heart to keep to the
  narrow way,
  to live according to Your will.

O God, You are good!

I have already experienced so much of Your goodness.

Let me also understand exactly what You want me to do.

Blatant liars are dragging my name through the dirt,
  but I continue, with all of my heart, to do what is right
  in Your sight.

Their consciences are dull. Everything you say deflects
  away from their ears;
  but your ordinances please me.

It was a joy to me when I finally recognized that I can't
  go on without you.

At that moment I realized how helpful your precepts are.

It's true--your law is priceless,

incomparably more valuable than mountains of gold.

Psalm 119, Stanza 9

Thanksgiving for Protection and Salvation

Sing a new song to the Lord, for he has performed wondrous deeds!

He, the holy God, has won the victory with his right arm.

All people of the earth will know, the Lord has saved Israel.

He has proven that we can rely on him.

He has kept his promises to remain merciful and faithful to his people.

To the ends of the earth, this news is impressive: God has redeemed Israel!

Praise the Lord, you people of earth!

Laud him with songs, sing and shout for joy!

Play to him on the harp, let the zither ring;

   honor the Lord with song!

Let trumpets and horns sound;

   praise God, your King.

Let the sea and all that dwells within it thunder and roar to honor him.

Let the whole earth break forth in celebration!

You rivers, clap your hands.

You mountains, praise our Lord

   for He comes to judge the earth.

His verdict is incorruptible and righteous.

Psalm 98

A Prayer for Anniversaries and Birthdays

Come, bless the Lord, all his servants,
   all who follow the ways of the Lord.

Lift up your hands in holy prayer,
   praise the Lord!

The Lord bless You.

May He who dwells on Mount Zion, the Maker of heaven
   and earth,
   bless all His servants.

Psalm 134

A Prayer for Holiness

Oh, how I love Your law;
    all day long I contemplate Your precepts.
I am wiser than my enemies;
    I understand more than my teachers
    because I continually meditate on Your ordinances.
Your wisdom gives me insight and discernment,
    superior even to the life experience of the elderly,
    because I have ordered my life according to your
    commandments.
I have never intentionally been crooked
    because it was always in my heart to follow your word.
I have willingly accepted your instruction
    for there is no teacher superior to you.
Your word is my favorite food,
    sweeter than honey.
Your law makes me wise and insightful,
    therefore I hate every form of falsehood.

Psalm 119, Stanza 13

A Prayer for Justice

The Lord alone is King!

Let the whole earth break out with joy;

let the far Islands be merry and mirthful.

Ominous dark clouds envelope Him;

righteousness and justice are the pillars of His power.

His prohibition against evil is fiery;

it surrounds His enemies with wasteland.

His lightning immerses the earth in bright light;

the whole earth sees it and trembles.

Mountains melt before Him like wax;

as do all the princes of the earth.

The heavens bear witness that he keeps His promises;

all the nations can see his majesty and might.

All those who worship idols and boast of their false gods'
power

will sink into the earth in shame.

For their idols will throw themselves down before the
Lord.

Joy governs Mount Zion;

the citizens of the city of Judah rejoice before you, O
God.

For you, Lord, are a righteous judge;

(continued next page)

Psalm 97

Yes, Lord, only you rule the whole world.
You are greater and more powerful than all other gods.

Do you love the Lord?
Then you must reject evil.
God protects all those who are faithful to him;
　he rescues them from the clutches of evildoers.
The one who obeys God lives in light;
　happiness fills those who are upright.
Indeed, rejoice in the Lord and give him thanks!
Remember what our Holy God has done for you.

Psalm 97

A Prayer for Knowledge of the Truth

L ord, Your word is eternal.

Even as the sun and stars were being formed,

already then, our word was applicable to all of life.

Your faithfulness is constant throughout all times and ages.

In faithfulness you created the earth.

Even as you called us into existence, Your constancy preceded us.

The heavens and the earth are here today

because You have ordained it.

Therefore everything exists to serve you.

Had your word not been the source of exceeding joy for me,

I would have perished in my desolation.

Never will I forget your commandments,

for they have strengthened me.

I belong to you, Lord. Please help me,

for I have ordered my life according to the precepts of Your word.

Conscienceless people have tried to deceive me,

but I daily renew my conviction to listen only to you.

I have seen that everything comes to an end in its time;

but your word endures forever.

Psalm 119, Stanza 12

A Prayer for Peace and Prosperity

Hear, oh please hear, Lord, what I desire to say to you:
    even if all I can do is sigh, please listen to me!
You are my King and my God;
    to you I cry out my heart.
In the early morning I bring you my commitment
and I pray because I know you hear me.
But, dear Lord, give me an answer!

You cannot remain silent before injustice.
You do not tolerate the godless in your presence.
You reject those who arrogantly mock you.
You loathe those who disregard your will.
You punish liars, murderers and hypocrites;
    they disgust You.

You have, however, permitted me to approach you
    because in your great mercy, you have accepted me.
With reverent awe I worship you in your sanctuary.
Show those who defame me that you stand by me.
I shall be faithful to you, as you are to me.
Help me to live according to your standards.

Psalm 5

My enemies scatter nothing but lies.

As evil and deceptive as they are, they cannot do anything else.

Death and doom accompany them.

Lord, bring them to justice!

Bring the same calamity on them they inflict on others.

Defy them! Absolutely nothing is sacred to them.

They rebel even against you!

But all who trust in you

will praise you in utmost happiness,

for in you they are secure.

Whoever loves you will exult with joy.

Whoever remains faithful to you,

will be graced with your peace and prosperity.

You surround them with your protective love.

Psalm 5

A Prayer to Find Purpose

I must confess--I belong to you, O God,

therefore I will do whatever you command.

With my whole heart, I desire to please you, Lord.

Please be merciful to me, as you have promised to be.

I have taken account of my life thus far,

and now I renew my commitment to obeying your commands.

I will not hesitate,

I will not delay following your orders.

The people who oppose and resist you want to cause my downfall,

but I will not neglect Your precepts.

In the middle of the night I awaken to thank you

because your judgements are right and just.

Whoever honors you, whoever lives by your precepts, is my friend.

Lord, through the world all of humanity can see your goodness and compassion.

Allow me to discern exactly what you want me to do.

Psalm 119, Stanza 8

A Prayer for Political Stability

All you people, applaud!
  Praise God with shouts of victory!
For the Lord is the most high God,
  a great King, who reigns over the earth.
Everyone will fear his power,
  everyone will fear us, His people.
He gave us victory, he gave us power to rule.
He has chosen our place for us—
  he makes us succeed and excel, for he loves us, his
  people.

The Lord God has ascended his throne
  accompanied by trumpet blasts and triumphant cheers.
Sing to his honor! Sing praises to our King!
For our God is King of the earth—
  understand this, and sing his praises.

Yes, God rules over all the nations.
He reigns from his throne, in holiness.
The rulers of the earth, the leaders of all governments
  have assembled
  with the chosen people of the God of Israel.
Shields and crests, all the symbols of their power, belong
  to God—
  he is the King of kings.
Only he is the exalted One!

Psalm 47

A Prayer for Righteousness

Sing to the Lord a new song;
  Sing to the Lord, all inhabitants of the earth!
Sing to the Lord and praise his name!
Proclaim, all day, every day, our God saves!
Tell the people of his majesty;
  make His wondrous deeds known to everyone.
For the Lord is great! Everyone shall extol Him.
He alone, of all the gods, is to be feared.
The people's idols are powerless figures,
  but our Lord created the heavens!
He emanates majesty and splendor,
  his strength and his loveliness fill his dwelling place,
  his holy temple.

Listen, all people: stand in awe before the Lord.
Submit to his governance.
Honor his great name, enter his temple and give
  obedience to him.
Bow down before him.
When he appears in His grandeur, with authority,
  the whole world will tremble in His presence.

Psalm 96

Say to the people: the Lord alone is King!
He laid the earth's foundation,
   it does not falter, does not give way.
He will judge all people with justice.
The heavens will rejoice,
   the earth will break forth in joy.
The sea and all it contains will thunder and roar.
The field and all that grows will delight.
Even the trees in the forest will cheer when the Lord
   appears,
   yes, when He comes to judge the earth.
His verdict is incorruptible and righteous.

Psalm 96

A Prayer for Success

L ord, my Protector, you have given me my life.
Please also give me the insight I need to live by your
standards.
All who honor and obey you will be pleased with me
because I rely on Your word.
O Lord, I know that your judgements are right.
Even when you have allowed me to experience the
darkest, most painful times,
you only had good in mind for me.
Please allow me to feel your compassion; comfort me
as you have promised to do.
It is my pleasure to keep your commandments.
Have mercy on me, and help me
so that I may again find joy in living.
Cause the downfall of all those who have without cause
plunged me into misery,
and I will forget them while I contemplate your rules.
My hope is that everyone who honors you,
all who live according to Your precepts,
will support me.
I am resolved to live my life according to your will,
so I will not fall into destruction.

Psalm 119, Stanza 10

A Prayer for Victory

When you are in great need, the Lord answers your prayer.

May the God of Israel protect you.

May He come to your aid from his sanctuary on Mount Zion.

He regards and respects the offerings you bring to him.

He accepts your sacrifice graciously.

May he grant your heartfelt desire.

May he permit your success in whatever good thing you resolve to accomplish.

When he has rescued you from your need,

we will exult in pleasure; we will wave banners of victory, and praise God.

May the Lord fulfill all your requests.

I know that the Lord helps his beloved one,

He answers him from his heavenly sanctuary.

He intervenes and rescues.

Some people swear by the power of their armed war machines,

by the fighting power of their soldiers.

We, however, trust in the power of the Lord our God.

They stagger and stumble, but we stand steady. We are immovable.

Lord help your loved ones;

please answer us when we cry out to you!

Psalm 20

A Prayer for Vindication

O God, please procure justice for me.

Defend me against all those who have contempt for everything holy.

Guard me from the influence of liars and swindlers,

for you are my protector.

Why, now, do I feel as if you have cast me aside?

Why must I suffer under the power of my enemies.

Grant me your light, your truth!

Lead me by the light of truth back to your holy mountain,

the temple of your presence.

I desire to worship before your altar.

I yearn to rejoice in you, to shout holy cheers of victory.

I will make music in gratitude to you, my God.

When I am unhappy,

when my heart is heavy,

I will hope in God.

I will certainly thank him once more.

He is my God; he will stand beside me!

Psalm 43

A Prayer to Overcome Anger

Lord, I can rely on you.
  Everything you determine is right and just.
Your commandments prove you are true to your holy nature;
  you adhere to truth.
I am beside myself with rage;
I see how my enemies trample your precepts.
Your word is reliable, therefore I love it.
I am unimportant and despised;
  yet I will never forget your word.
Your righteous judgments are eternal;
  your law is pure truth.
Even when I tremble in fear, even when I see no way out of trouble,
  I find joy in your commandments.
Your precepts are just; therefore I have no desire
  to contend with or change them.
Please help me to more fully comprehend them
  that I may be refreshed and restored.

Psalm 119, Stanza 18

A Prayer to Overcome Anxiety

L ord, I am not arrogant:

I don't believe my needs are more important than anyone else's;

I don't concern myself with things that are too difficult for me;

I don't presume to fathom the secrets of the universe.

I have composed and quieted my soul.

My thoughts are peaceful;

my heart is content.

I am like a child resting in its mother's arms.

Let's trust that God will take care of us, now and forever.

Psalm 131

A Prayer for Guidance

L ord, I yearn for you!

My God, I have put all my faith in you;

do not cast me aside now!

Do not grant my enemies this triumph over me.

I know this: no one who hopes in you will fail,

but the one who is disloyal and frivolous, the one who departs from you, will stumble and fall.

Lord, please show me the course I should take.

Indicate what you want me to do.

Step by step, let me experience your staunch faithfulness.

You are my God who helps me,

you have always been my one and only hope.

Consider how you have already proved your compassion

and your love for me.

Forgive the sins of my youth;

forget my wanton delinquency.

Remember instead your compassionate nature

and be merciful to me!

The Lord is right and good.

That is the reason he leads the one who has wandered away from him

back to the right path.

(continued next page)

Psalm 25

To all who confess their guilt,
  he shows how they should live and what he expects.
In love and faithfulness he leads everyone
  who keeps his law and commandments.
Lord, please be true to your reputation;
  forgive my great debt.

And what becomes of the person who obeys the Lord?

The Lord shows him the right way.
To the obedient he gives happiness and abundance;
  their descendants will inherit the land.
The Lord opens the eyes of all who believe in him,
  all who take his word seriously;
  he clarifies meaning for them.
He allows them to know the reason he made a covenant
  with his people.

Psalm 25

A Prayer to Overcome Depression

Lord, I can't sink any lower.
From the depths of my despair I cry out to you--
I plead with you; please hear my prayer!

If you counted every wrong everyone has committed,
   no one could approach you to stand in your presence.
But we find forgiveness in you.
You graciously forgive so that we will learn to revere you
with heartfelt awe.

I place my entire hope in the Lord;
   I wait for the Lord with greater anticipation
   than the night watchman waits for dawn.

Oh, Israel, put your hope in the Lord.
His love never fails;
   his abundant saving power overflows.
He himself will free us from the bondage of our sins and
   failures.

Psalm 130

A Prayer to Overcome Discouragement

Lord, your law is exceedingly marvelous,

therefore I gladly obey you.

The light of insight enters our lives when we begin to
revere your word.

People who formerly lived in foolishness and ignorance

become wise when they follow your precepts.

My yearning for your guidance is stronger than my thirst
for water on a sultry day.

Lord, please regard me graciously,

for you have promised compassion to all who love you.

Protect me from evil and strengthen me in the face of
temptation,

because I believe in you.

Rescue me from those who seek to oppress me,

for if they succeed, my service to you will be hindered.

Allow me to experience your goodness;

show me how to live according to your will.

When I see how people despise and scoff at your wisdom,

my sorrow overwhelms me--I cannot stop weeping.

Psalm 119, Stanza 17

A Prayer to Overcome Envy

D on't let troublemakers fill you with indignation.

Don't let evildoers make you envious of their success.

For they will wither like the grass.

Like flowers, they will shrivel and fade.

Rely on the Lord, and do good.

Abide by the covenant God has made with Israel and adhere to the truth, always.

Be happy in the Lord;

know that he will satisfy your deepest desires.

Trust in the Lord, do not worry about your future.

Commit all your ways to God and he will see to it that you increase in righteousness.

As dawn overcomes the darkness, his goodness will increase in you

until you shine like the noonday sun.

His faithfulness will be undeniable;

his perfect goodness will be clearly visible.

Wait patiently for the Lord's intervention.

Do not be filled with indignation if people conspire to do evil and appear successful.

Do not allow fury and rage to overpower you,

(continued next page)

Psalm 37

for if you become too upset your emotions will lead you into wrong doing.

God will exterminate the evil doers,

but those who trust in the Lord will inherit the earth.

Before long, the wicked will vanish.

You will wonder where they have gone,

no trace of them will remain.

And then, those who have renounced violence will inherit the earth.

They will live in perfect health and happiness.

The wicked grit their teeth and devise evil plans against all who are faithful to God,

but the Lord laughs at them because he knows their day of reckoning is coming.

The wicked draw their swords and aim their arrows; they want to murder the defenseless and oppressed, to eliminate all who sincerely believe in God.

But their swords pierce their own hearts and their bows shatter into splinters.

It is preferable to possess very little and do God's will

than to live in the lap of luxury and despise God.

For the Lord allows the power-hungry to founder and fail,

but he lovingly cares for all who are faithful to him.

He provides for them day by day,

they remain continuously in possession of his promises.

In times of destitution they will not die forever.

Psalm 37

Even in the greatest famine, the Lord will satisfy their
  hunger.

The wicked, however, will perish eternally.

The Lord's enemies will vanish suddenly, as prairie
  flowers fade and are blown away,

  they will disappear like smoke.

The unscrupulous borrow money and never repay

  but the one who listens to God is cheerfully charitable.

The people blessed by God will inherit the earth;

  but those cursed by God will be eradicated.

When people are able to resolutely walk with God,

  then they owe it to God to be thankful, for God loves
  them.

And if they stumble, they will not fall to the ground,

  for the Lord will help them regain steadiness.

And in my old age, when I look back on my long life I
  will see,

  God never abandoned anyone who loved him.

The children of the faithful did not have to beg for their
  bread.

On the contrary, those who love God could lend much
  and give away their wealth

  and their children, too, were much blessed by God.

Avoid wicked people; do good deeds--

(continued next page)

Psalm 37

then your descendants will always abide under the protection of God's promises.

For the Lord loves righteousness and justice.

He will never forsake those who revere him.

He will protect them forever,

but he will annihilate the descendants of the wicked.

All who trust in the Lord will live forever

under the protection of God's promised faithfulness.

The one who depends on God will speak words of wisdom and justice.

He carries God's law in his heart,

he never strays from the narrow way.

On the other hand, there are those who wish to contradict God, taking every opportunity to overpower and condemn people who listen to God.

But the Lord does not allow innocent people to fall forever into the hands of the wicked.

He does not allow anyone to be unjustly punished eternally.

So hope in the Lord and keep his commandments.

Then you will be honored;

he will make you the recipient of all his promises.

You will see how he exterminates the wicked.

I saw a wicked man, a tyrant as mighty as a deeply-rooted oak,

he dominated the landscape.

Psalm 37

Some time later I went back there;

he had vanished.

I looked for him and found no trace.

Pay attention to people who are sincere and faithful.

You will see, well into the future, they are living in tranquility.

But the people who renounce God will perish;

eternal death is their certain consequence.

The Lord stands by those who strive to do his will.

He comforts and strengthens them in times of extreme need.

In him is help and salvation.

Indeed, he rescues us from the wicked and stands beside us when we seek refuge in him.

Psalm 37

A Prayer to Overcome Fear

L ord I implore you to answer my prayer!
I am determined to live by your precepts.

I plead with you to help me!

I want to obey your commandments.

Before dawn breaks I am already crying out to you for help.

I have placed all my confidence, every last shred of my hope in your word.

All night long I contemplate what you have revealed to us.

Hear my prayer, for I trust in your lovingkindness.

Please allow your righteous ordinances to renew my strength--

wicked people surround me to overpower and harm me.

Surely you can see how far they have removed themselves from your law.

But you are near to me, Lord.

I can trust in your every word.

I have immersed myself in the study of your precepts;

I have recognized that your righteous word endures for eternity.

Psalm 119, Stanza 19

A Prayer to Overcome Frustration

Lord, I have campaigned for you and defended your ways.

Please make your promises come true,

for I trust in them.

Always, in my greatest need, your assurances have revived me.

Complacent, self-righteous people continually speak evil of me

and still I keep to the narrow way, following your precepts.

I have never lost courage because I remind myself that you have always provided what is right and good for me.

When I consider the people who distance themselves from you and your ordinances, it infuriates me.

My life on this earth is so brief;

but for as long as I live I will extol the wisdom of your precepts.

Even in the middle of the night I think of you, Lord;

following your ordinances is becoming my deeply ingrained habit.

Time and again it pleases me

to unswervingly walk the narrow way with you.

Psalm 119, Stanza 7

A Prayer to Express Gratitude

Praise the Lord, all you people;

Honor him, all you tribes and nations.

For he loves us with a strong and mighty love,

and his faithfulness never ends.

Hallelujah!

Psalm 117

A Prayer to Overcome Guilt

On Mount Zion you may be found, O God—
  if people silently adore you, if they sing hymns to praise you,
if they keeps the promises they have made.
Because you listen to prayers, your people seek you.

A heavy guilt overwhelms me,
  and yet, despite my unfaithfulness, you will forgive me.

Happy and blessed are all whom you have chosen,
  who are allowed to enter into your holy sanctuary.
There, in your temple, you bless us with goodness,
  you satisfy our deepest desires.

For You, O God, are faithful.
When we need your help, you answer us with miracles.
You are the hope of all people, even to the ends of the earth.
You have formed the mountains by your might.
Your power is visible to everyone.
You calm the roaring seas;
You silence the thundering waves.
Yes, you also silence the multitudes and the mobs,
  all the people of the earth stand in awe of your fierce power.

(continued next page)

Psalm 65

From east to west the nations rejoice in you.

You care for the soil of the earth,

   you enrich the soil and make it fruitful.

You provide an abundance of water so grains grow profusely.

You moisten the plowed fields with rain.

You soak the parched earth and cause the plants to flourish.

You generously give a plentiful harvest--the crown of the year.

The prairies bloom,

   the hills rejoice.

Grazing herds are dense in the fields while grains undulate in the valleys.

Everything shimmers in exultation;

   yes, all creation sings.

Psalm 65

A Prayer for Times of Indecision

L ord, I am devastated;
   please renew my strength as you have promised.
I have repeatedly come to you with my needs
   and you have always helped me.
Please show me again, now, what I should do.
Help me to understand your ordinances,
help me to contemplate all the wonders chronicled in
   your word.
I weep endlessly in my sorrow.
Lift me up again, according to your promises.
Whenever I am tempted to stray from you,
   please stand between me and my error;
   stand by me and give me clear instructions.
I am determined to remain true to you,
   therefore I will always hold before my eyes
   that which you have proclaimed to be right and good.
I will hold unflinchingly to your precepts.
Lord, please do not permit my steadfast conviction to be
   turned into mockery.
Help me to walk the narrow way with single-minded
   determination,
for your ordinances point out that if I follow your ways,
   my future will contain happiness and joy.

Psalm 119, Stanza 4

A Prayer to Express Joy

I will praise the Lord with all my heart.
  Lord, my God, how great you are!
You are clothed in majesty and glory;
  you are cloaked in pure light.
You spread the heavens like a tent;
  you establish your dwelling above the clouds.
Indeed the clouds are like your chariot;
  you ride therein on the wings of the wind.
Wind and weather are your messengers;
  lightning bolts are your servants.

You grounded the earth on a solid foundation, unshakable
  for all ages.
Like a garment, the ancient seas concealed the continents.
The primal water mass covered the highest mountains.
They shrank back when You shouted.
They fled from your thundering voice.
The mountains rose and the valley sank in the places You
  determined.

You established the sea's boundaries, which it was not
  allowed to overstep.
Never again shall it engulf the whole earth.
You made the headwaters gush into the valleys,
  to find their way between mountains,

Psalm 104

to water the animals of the plains,
   to quench the wild donkey's thirst.
Birds nest along the shores;
   in dense foliage they sing their songs.
You make rain to fall on the mountains;
   the earth soaks it in and grows fruitful.

You make grass to grow for the grazing animals;
   you make plants to nourish people.
They plough, plant and harvest;
   they have wine to cheer them,
   oil to groom the body,
   bread to nourish.

But you, Lord, planted the giant cedars of Lebanon
   and you give them enough rain.
In their branches the birds build their nests;
   storks tend their young in the boughs of the Cypress.
The high hills are the mountain goats' territory;
   the groundhog shelters in the fields.
You have created the moon to determine the months
   and the sun knows exactly when to set.
You make the darkness break in, night comes
   and in the forest thickets, creatures stir.

(continued next page)

Psalm 104

The young lions roar after prey;

from you, O God, they await their sustenance.

Then, as soon as the sun rises, the night prowlers creep

back to their burrows and their hiding places.

And people rise to go to their work,

occupied until evening comes.

O Lord, what immeasurable diversity your works exhibit;

there are countless indications of your wisdom.

The whole earth is filled with your creatures!

There is the ocean, so endlessly great and wide;

its species are innumerable,

from enormous to microscopic.

Ships pass over sea monsters frolicking in the depths,

creatures you made for your pleasure.

All your creatures wait for you to provide food at the right time.

They accept what You allocate;

you open your hand and they are richly satisfied.

But if you turn away from them, they fear for their lives;

they die and return to dust when you take their breath away.

And when you give them breath, by your Spirit they come to life;

and so you recreate and replenish the earth.

Psalm 104

May the power and glory of the Lord remain forever
with us.

May he rejoice in his creation.

When he glances at the earth, it trembles;

when he touches the mountains, they smoke.

I will sing to the Lord for as long as I live;

I will make music to God my whole life long.

How happy I am in the Lord. May my songs please him.

It is true that all who oppose him will perish,

all that they build will vanish entirely,

but I will always praise the Lord with all my heart.

Hallelujah!

Psalm 104

A Prayer for Times of Loneliness

Our sovereign Lord,
    how great and glorious is your name.
Heaven and earth testify to your power.
Your praise, sung from the mouths of children
    drowns out Your enemies' curses--
    their vindictiveness grows slack,
    they are abashed into silence.

I look to heaven and see what your hand has
accomplished--
    the moon and the stars!
You have sketched out the trajectory for all of them.

How small and insignificant is a human,
    and yet you watch over us.
We are minuscule and still You care for us.
You have raised humanity up as the crown of Your
creation.
You have clothed us in lofty dignity.
Only your honor is greater.

Psalm 8

You have commissioned us to rule over your creation.
You have laid all at our feet--
   the sheep and cattle,
   the animals of the prairie and tundra,
   the birds in the sky and the fish in the vast sea.

Oh, sovereign Lord,
how great and glorious is your name.
Heaven and earth testify to your power.

Psalm 8

A Prayer for Times of Weariness

L ord, I implore you to answer my prayer!
I am determined to live by your precepts.

I plead with you to help me!

I do want to obey your commandments.

Before dawn breaks I am already crying out to you for help.

I have placed all my confidence, every last shred of my hope in your word.

All night long I contemplate what you have revealed to me.

Hear my prayer, for I trust in your loving kindness.

Please allow Your righteous ordinances to renew my strength--

wicked people surround me to overpower and harm me.

Surely you can see how far they have removed themselves from your law.

But you are near to me, Lord.

I can trust in your every word.

I have immersed myself in the study of your precepts;

I have recognized that your righteous word endures for eternity.

Psalm 119, Stanza 14

A Prayer for Worrisome Times

L ord, I thank you with all my heart.

I praise only you; no other gods do I honor.

I bow down before you in your holy sanctuary;

I praise your loving faithfulness,

for you have fulfilled all your promises,

even beyond my expectations.

When I cried to you for help,

you heard me, you renewed my strength.

All the rulers of the world will thank you, Lord,

when they learn that your word is trustworthy.

They will sing of your deeds,

for your power and glory are exceedingly great.

Yet, despite your greatness, you care intimately for the weak and humble;

but from a distance, you overlook those who are arrogant.

Even when I am surrounded by troubles

you protect me from the wrath of my enemies,

you rescue me by your strength.

Truly, Lord, you will care for me in the future also,

for your lovingkindness is boundless and endless.

You have created me, Lord; I am yours.

Please do not ever abandon me.

Psalm 138

A Prayer for Confidence

Favored and comforted are those of whom no evil can be spoken,

who comply with God's ordinances.

Favored and comforted are those who keep his precepts,

who serve him wholeheartedly.

They do no wrong for they live according to his will.

Your decrees, O Lord, should be carefully observed by everyone.

I long for increased understanding so that I may keep your ordinances.

I hold your commands ever before my eyes,

that I may never live in shame,

that I might praise you with a sincere heart.

I am learning your law ever more completely.

I want to keep your precepts.

Help me, please. Do not forsake me.

Psalm 119, Stanza 1

A Prayer for Consolation

The Lord is my Shepherd, I will lack nothing.

He pastures me in soft, peaceful meadows.

He leads me to fresh springs.

He renews my strength.

He guides me along safe paths to demonstrate his faithful goodness.

And even when I walk in dark valleys in the presence of death, I will not be afraid

because You, Lord, are beside me.

Your shepherd's staff is my comforting protection.

You invite me to the table you prepared for me;

my enemies are forced to recognize my blessings.

You greet me like the master of the house greets an honored guest,

anointing me with oil.

You give abundantly--my cup overflows!

I am certain your goodness and love will accompany me my whole life long,

and I will dwell in your house forever.

Psalm 23

A Prayer for Courage

Lord, will you show me again how much you love me--
please help me as you have promised,
that I may give the appropriate response
to those who right now despise me.
I trust that you always keep your word.
In your word I have placed all my hopes.
Please do not allow me to be embarrassed into silence,
for how, then, could I extol your faithfulness.
You have granted me immense freedom in living
because I have continually delved into the wisdom of
your precepts.
Even in front of kings and rulers, without timidity,
I will argue that your word is irrefutably valuable.
With great pleasure I adhere to your ordinances
because I love them.
I yearn for your word, it is precious to me;
and I carefully consider all that you have decreed.

Psalm 119, Stanza 6

A Prayer for Faith

God, you are my God!
 I long for you; I need you!
Like a withered prairie thirsts for rain, I thirst for you, O
  God.
I seek you in your holy sanctuary;
  I want to see your power and your glory.
Your love is more important to me than my very life!

Therefore let me praise you:
  I will thank you my whole life long;
  I will raise up my hands in prayer.
I sing joyfully to you, I praise you.
My soul is satisfied in your presence,
  your nearness is like a festive banquet to me.
Rejoicing, I give you praise.

At night when I rest in my bed, I contemplate your ways.
All my thoughts are of you.
Because you have always helped me, I praise you.
I am safe and secure because you protect me.
I bind myself to you and you hold me in your strong
  hand.

(continued next page)

Psalm 63

Those who seek to destroy my life will themselves all die.

They will not escape your wrath.

Nothing will be left of them.

Praise you, Lord, for choosing me.

I am happy and blessed because you stand with me.

The one who serves God with complete obedience can take pride in his faith.

He can be confident that the mouths of liars will be silenced.

Psalm 63

A Prayer for Forgiveness

L ord, will you make me experience your wrath?
   I beseech you, do not punish me any longer!
Have mercy on me, Lord, I'm tired to the bone and can't
   endure any more.
Give me strength again, renew my courage,
   for I am utterly exhausted.
I don't understand anything anymore.
Lord, how long will you stand by just watching?
Please attend to my needs once more. Help me!
Because you are a merciful God;
   be merciful to me and rescue me.
If I die, I will not be able to thank you.
How could I praise you from the grave?

Oh, I am so weary of sighing.
At night I weep like a child until my pillow is soaked
   and my eyes are swollen.
I have collaborated with your enemies;
   my guilt has caused me sorrow.
I feel cornered, surrounded by malice and meanness.

(continued next page)

Psalm 6

Flee and disperse, my guilt! For I know the Lord has seen my tears.

He has heard my cry and accepted my supplication.

The enemies of the Lord have run out of luck. They can no longer harass me.

They will be shamed, for I have been pardoned.

A Prayer for Sustenance

I will honor you, my God and King!

I will praise you for all eternity.

Daily I will bless your name, everywhere.

Great is the Lord! Everyone should praise Him.

His greatness is incomprehensible.

Each generation will proclaim to the next

   your great deeds, to tell their children of your mighty acts.

May your power and glory be proclaimed by everyone!

I will speak of your miracles,

   and contemplate your wonders.

Again and again people will tell the stories of your amazing goodness;

   they will tell of your great righteousness,

   they will praise your faithfulness.

The Lord is merciful and compassionate.

His patience is endless; his love is boundless.

The Lord is good to all; he showers kindness on all His creatures.

Therefore all creation shall praise you!

All who love you shall honor you;

   they shall proclaim the greatness of your sovereignty.

(continued next page)

Psalm 145

They shall tell how you have demonstrated your power,
  how glorious is your reign.

Your kingdom is everlasting, enduring from generation
  to generation.

The word of the Lord is reliable;
  his deeds are gracious and loving.
He helps those who have no strength left;
  he lifts up the fallen.

Every living being looks to you in hope,
  and you give to all of them food at the right time.
You open your hand and satisfy all your creatures;
  you meet all needs.

The Lord is right in everything he does;
  we can rely on him.
The Lord is near to those who pray to him,
  those who sincerely call on him.
He satisfies the desires of those who honor him;
  he hears their cries for help and he rescues them.
God protects those who love him; but those who want
  nothing to do with him, he destroys.
I will praise the Lord, and every living thing will bless
  him forever.
He is the holy one, our God.

Psalm 145

A Prayer for Patience

I wait expectantly for your help, O Lord;

 I am withering in my impatience.

When will you fulfill your promises to me?

When will you comfort me?

I feel useless, as old and used up as a cracked wine barrel,

 and still I never grow weary of following your precepts.

How long must I wait?

 When will You finally pass judgement

 against those who ridicule me and hinder me?

These mockers, these arrogant people have dug a grave for me.

 They are indifferent to Your wisdom.

Help me, please! They persecute me for no good reason.

 Yet, I will rely on Your commandments.

I steadfastly refuse to go against Your word,

 even when my enemies torture and torment me to the point of death.

Please be merciful to me and let me live,

 so that I may continue to serve You according to Your will.

Psalm 119 stanza 11

A Prayer for Times of Confusion

How blessed are those who do not listen
  to advice from people who know nothing of God.
Blessed are those who do not follow the example
  of people who violate God's will.
Blessed are those who keep away
  from people who have contempt for everything holy.
Happy and blessed are those who delight
  in the law of the Lord and ponder it day and night.
They are like a tree planted near the water;
  it yearly bears fruit and its leaves never shrivel.
They successfully carries out their good intentions.
All those who are apathetic about God fare quite differently, however--
  They are like arid foliage, wizened and scattered by wind.
  They are failures; they cannot stand before God's judgement.
  Because they have renounced him, they are cast out from God's community.
The Lord looks after all those who live according to his word.
But those who defiantly shut God out of their lives
  run headlong into their own destruction.

Psalm 1

A Prayer for Health

I want to praise you, exalted God,

for you have lifted me up out of the depths!

You did not allow my enemies to rejoice over my misfortune.

Lord, my God!

To you I cried for help, and you healed me.

I was more dead than alive,

but you wrested me from the arms of death

and gave me the gift of new life.

Sing your songs to the Lord,

all you who have experienced his loving kindness.

Thank him and testify--he is the holy God of Israel!

His anger grazes us for only a moment

but his goodness endures our whole lives long.

If, in the evening, we are sorrowful and weepy,

in the morning we will once again be able to rejoice in happiness.

When I was prosperous and lived in security, I thought,

"What could possibly happen to me?"

For you, Lord, had placed me atop a strong rock.

I had your goodness to thank for all my fortune.

But then you turned away from me;

(continued next page)

Psalm 30

I was shocked, dismayed, horrified.
I beseeched you for mercy, I cried out to you,
   "What good would my death be to you?
Can a dead person thank you?
Can a dead person boast of your faithfulness?
Lord, hear my prayer! Have mercy on me and help me!"

You transformed my lament into a dance of joy.
You took off my garments of mourning;
   you arrayed me in celebration clothes.
Now I can praise you with my songs.
Never will I keep silent;
   I will openly declare what you have done for me.
Always and forever, I want to thank you, my Lord and
   my God!

Psalm 30

A Prayer for Mercy

Hear me, O Lord, and please answer me,
for I am broken down and helpless.
Rescue my life, for I belong to you.
I trust in you to help me.

You are my God; I am your servant,
therefore please be merciful to me, Lord.
I cry out to you all day long.
Grant me renewed gladness.
I yearn for you!

You are good, Lord, and ready to forgive.
Your lovingkindness toward all who pray to you is
immeasurable.
Lord, I implore you, hear my prayer.
I am desperate.
I cry to you -- I know you will hear me.

There is no other god like you, Lord;
no one can accomplish what you do.
You have created all people;
they will come to you,
they will bow before you and honor you,
for you are great and powerful; a God who performs
miracles.

(continued next page)

Psalm 86

You alone are God; there is no other.

Lord, please show me your way.
I want to be faithful to you, to obey you.
Grant me just this one desire;
   you to honor and you to obey.
With my whole heart I will thank you, Lord, my God;
   I will praise you.
Your love for me is boundless.
You have saved me from disaster and certain death.

Arrogant people conspire against me.
They ally themselves together;
   they champion hatred, outrage and violence--
   they plan to do me in.
They want nothing to do with your ways, Lord.

But you are a gracious and compassionate God.
Your patience is immense.
Your love and your faithfulness are endless.
Turn to me, please, and have mercy. Help me!

Lord, please show me a sign of your lovingkindness.
Then all who despise me will be ashamed
   because you, Lord God, have helped and comforted
  me.

Psalm 86

A Prayer for Perseverance

L ord, please reveal to me the wisdom of your precepts. I want to observe them my whole life long.

Give me insight, that I may keep your ordinances.

I am determined to abide by them.

Help me to fulfill your commands,

so that pleasing you becomes my pleasure.

Instill in me a deep love for your word,

and do not allow me to become greedy.

I want nothing to do with any mindless, trashy amusement or endeavor.

Please help me to delight in doing your will.

Lord, you always fulfill your promises!

I know they apply to me, to all who esteem and honor your word.

People will laugh at me, and insult my childlike trust in you.

Please protect me, help me persevere in doing your will;

because whatever you desire for me is always good.

I yearn to be fully obedient to your instructions.

As you fulfill your promises to me, I will be encouraged.

Psalm 119, Stanza 5

A Prayer for Powerful Influence

Hallelujah, praise the Lord.

I will bless the Lord; I will praise him my life long.

I will sing to honor him all the days of my life.

Do not put your trust in people of influence, those who wield power.

They are only mortals like you; they cannot save you.

They, too, will die. All of their grand plans will vanish with them.

Blessed are those who look to God for help.

Blessed are those who trust in the Lord, the maker of heaven and earth.

He made the sea and all that dwells in it.

He never breaks his promises.

To the oppressed, he brings justice.

To the hungry, he gives food.

He sets prisoners free.

The Lord gives sight to the blind;

  he lifts up the downtrodden.

He offers protection to sojourners in foreign lands;

  he provides care and comfort to orphans and widows.

Psalm 146

Those who honor and revere him will experience His
lovingkindness,

but those who disobey him,

will wander without him, lost in the confusion and
chaos they make for themselves.

The Lord rules forever, eternally.

Our God will reign for all ages.

Hallelujah.

Psalm 146

A Prayer for Strength

Praise the Lord, O my soul;

let all that I am extol his holy name.

Praise the Lord and do not forget all the good things he has done:

he forgives all my sins and heals all my sicknesses;

he shields me from death and renews my life;

he crowns my life with lovingkindness and compassion;

throughout my life he blesses me with overflowing goodness and abundance;

he makes me feel young, strong as a soaring eagle.

The Lord keeps His word:

he aids the oppressed;

he gives them the justice He has promised;

he confided in Moses and showed Israel all his mighty deeds.

He has done great things!

The Lord is compassionate and full of lovingkindness:

his patience is great and His love is boundless;

he does not blame us endlessly and does not remain angry forever;

he does not punish us as we deserve;

he does not count our sins and failures against us.

For as high as the heavens rise above the earth

so great is his love for all who reverently approach him.

Psalm 103

As far as east is from west,

   he separates us from our guilt.

As a father loves his children,

the Lord loves all who honor him.

He knows how fragile we are; he does not forget that we are as dust.

Humans are like the grass blooming in the field.

When the desert wind blows the grass vanishes without a trace

   and no one remembers where it blossomed.

The goodness of the Lord, however, endures forever

   for all who obey Him.

Our descendants, if they keep his covenant, if they follow his commandments, shall receive the blessings of his promises.

The Lord has established his throne in heaven,

He rules as King over all the earth.

Praise the Lord, you mighty angels who heed his word and obey his orders.

Praise the Lord, you heavenly beings who carry out his instructions.

Praise the Lord, all His creation, for all are under his authority!

And I, too, shall praise the Lord with all my heart.

Psalm 103

A Prayer for Wisdom

Hallelujah, praise the Lord!

I will thank the Lord with all my heart in the presence of his faithful ones,

yes, before the congregation.

What the Lord has accomplished is tremendous.

Whoever rejoices in his deeds always remembers--

his works are spectacular and unrivaled.

Whatever God has promised, he will fulfill forever.

He himself has insured that his wonders will never sink into oblivion.

The Lord is gracious and compassionate to those who honor and obey him.

He provides them with plenty to eat.

He never forgets the covenant he made with Israel.

He proved to them his power.

He gave the land of other nations to them.

In all that he does, he is trustworthy and just.

We can rely, with confidence, on his precepts.

Their relevance never changes,

they remain valid forever.

Psalm 111

Holy and fearsome is our God.
Wisdom begins when we take seriously his every word.

The one who aligns his life according to God's ordinances
is the one who obtains discernment.

God's praises shall never be silenced.

Psalm 111

A Prayer for When You Feel Abandoned

I call to God, indeed, I cry out again and again,
   until he hears my voice.
I have terrifying fears;
   I see no way out.
I pray to God ceaselessly,
   even in the middle of the night I reach out to him.

I am comfortless.
When I think of God, I sigh.
When I consider my situation, I lose heart.
I cannot sleep.
My worries keep me awake.
I am tormented by anxiety until I find no words to
   describe my hopeless condition.

I remember earlier times,
   I think of years long past
   when I played the harp, when I was able to be joyful.
Every night I think too much,
   my heart grows heavy,
   my thoughts spiral around the same questions:
   Has the Lord abandoned me forever?
   Will he never again show friendship to me?
   Will I forever be deprived of His mercy?

Psalm 77

Are his promises now invalid?
Has he forgotten to be gracious to me?
Why has he shut his heart to me in anger?

This is what pains me most:
  God, the Most High, seems to conduct himself differently
    than before--
  it appears he no longer takes up my cause!

Lord, I remember your great deeds;
  I consider the wonders you accomplished.
I recall what you have done;
  again and again, I remember.
O God, all Your works are holy;
  there is no other god as powerful as you!
You alone are the God who accomplishes greatness;
  you allow the people to experience your power.
By your strength, you freed your people, the descendants
    of Jacob and Joseph,
  from the prison of Egypt.
Whey they saw the swirling floods of water
  the depths of the seas shook.
Steaming rain poured from the clouds,
  powerful thunderclaps crashed,

(continued next page)

Psalm 77

your lightning bolts split the air.
In the storm, your voice thundered;
   glaring lightning electrified the earth;
   everything trembled and quaked.
You charted a course through the sea.
Your path led through mighty floodwaters,
   yet no one could see you.
By Moses and Aaron, your servants,
   like a shepherd you led your people.

Psalm 77

A Prayer for When You've Been Accused

O my God, surely you can see how beat down
  and despondent I am?
Please help me, for I have never lost sight of your love.
Will you be my advocate and counsel?
Please take my case
  for only you can assure my acquittal.
I am counting on your promise to rescue me.

Those who defy you cannot expect you to come to their
  aid,
  because they have been indifferent to your counsel,
  refusing to abide by your instructions for living.

Lord, you have so often demonstrated your lovingkindness to me;
  please renew my courage again,
  please make a fair and just determination.

Many enemies persecute and hassle me;
  still I have not deserted the path you ordained for me,
  still I have followed your commands.

You see who loathes me, who is disgusted by me--
  those who are unfaithful to you, who defy your word.

(continued next page)

Psalm 119, Stanza 20

But I, Lord, love your commandments;
   therefore show me your love and renew my joy in living.

Every word you utter is true.
All of your judgements and decisions, Lord,
   will endure forever.

Psalm 119, Stanza 20

A Prayer for When You've Been Betrayed

Lord, I plead with you:

rescue me, come quickly to my aid.

Whoever seeks my downfall will fail,

he will be publicly unmasked.

Whoever maliciously rejoices over my misfortune, you will hunt down,

you will clothe him in reproaches and disgrace.

And if people gloatingly gossip about me to ruin my reputation, saying, "Ha-ha!"

they will sheepishly slink away

when their self-inflicted disgrace is exposed.

And all who put their trust in you, Lord, will cheer for joy!

The person who knows your judgments, the one who loves you,

will continually profess, "Great is the Lord!"

I am helpless. I depend on you, Lord.

Take care of me, for you are my only help;

you are my Savior.

Come quickly, my God. Don't hesitate any longer!

Psalm 70

A Prayer for Times of Calamity and Disaster

I lift my eyes to the hills,
  remembering the unfailing source of my help—
  my help comes from the Lord, the creator of heaven
  and earth.

The Lord will not permit me to stumble or fall;
  he is my guardian who never sleeps.
Indeed, the protector of Israel never slumbers.

The Lord watches over me;
  he is as near as my shadow.
In the daytime the sun will not scorch me;
  in the night the moonlight will not impair me.

The Lord stands between me and calamity;
  he preserves my life.
He watches over my coming and going.
He is standing beside me, now and forever.

Psalm 121

A Prayer against Pressure to Conform

L ord, influential and powerful people,
  who have no right to control me, are hassling me,
  but the only commands I pay attention to,
  are those you have spoken.
I find as much pleasure in your word
  as someone who discovers a hidden treasure.
I detest hateful lies
  but I love your law.
I praise you seven times a day, Lord,
  because your judgements are good and just.
Those who love and abide by your laws live in peace;
  they will never sink.
Lord, I put my hope in your saving power
  for I have oriented me life according to your precepts.
Your instructions are the only standard for my behavior;
  I have treasured them in my heart, I have committed
  them to memory.
Yes, I earnestly follow your commands and instructions
  because you thoroughly know me,
  you see my every thought, my every word, my every
  deed.

Psalm 119, Stanza 21

A Prayer for Times of Doubt

Lord, how can young people live without incurring guilt?

By aligning their lives according to Your precepts.

I wish to be faithful to you;

don't let me stray from the path

you have ordained me to walk.

I impress your word deeply in my consciousness

that I might not offend you.

I want to thank and praise you, Lord.

Please teach me to always adhere to your ordinances.

I constantly repeat your instructions to myself.

I treasure your commands like vast wealth.

I contemplate your instructions and follow them.

Your laws make me glad;

I will never forget your word.

Psalm 119, Stanza 2

A Prayer Against Harassment

L ord, I plead with you to hear me!

Permit me an ever-deepening understanding of your word.

Please hear my cry and rescue me according to your promise.

My heart overflows with praise for you;

I sing joyfully because you have allowed me to recognize wisdom in Your precepts.

To extol your word gladdens me;

everything you command is good.

Please intervene. Please help me!

I have chosen to abide by your law, to let it be my one standard.

I yearn for your assistance, O Lord;

help me do Your will. Your precepts are my greatest treasure!

Give me long life that I may praise you more,

and allow your wise ordinances to aid me

when I wander around like a homeless sheep who has lost his Shepherd.

Seek and find me Lord, because I belong to you.

I will not forget your instructions.

Psalm 119, Stanza 22

A Prayer for When You've Been Insulted

L ord, I am your servant; please meet all my needs.

For only if I am free from pressing want

can I live to obey Your word.

Open my eyes that I may recognize the wonders contained in your precepts.

The world will not be my dwelling place forever,

therefore I need your ordinances to show me

what is right in Your eyes, to reveal

the narrow way that leads to you.

This is my great yearning:

to more deeply understandyYour wisdom.

You punish the self-righteous and curse those who violate your laws.

And because I direct my life according to your precepts,

those people shower me with derision and ridicule.

Please put an end to the scoffing

of those who sit together forging plans against me.

I will serve you always,

thinking only of your precepts,

delighting always in your ordinances,

for these are the counsels of wisdom.

Psalm 119, Stanza 3

A Prayer for Times of Injury, Illness or Death

Protect me, my God, for I trust in you.

You are my Lord, my entire happiness and good fortune,

therefore I am happy to be surrounded by people,

who live according to your will.

They are a good influence.

But all those who turn away from the living God

to run after idols, will see no end to their troubles.

I will bring no sacrifice, I will give no service to these false gods.

I will not even name them.

You, Lord, are everything to me--

you give me all I need.

My future lies in your hands.

Whatever you give to me is good.

Whatever you appoint for me is pleasing.

I praise the Lord, for he helps me arrive at good decisions.

Day and night my thoughts are of him.

I look to the Lord at all times.

He stands beside me to keep me from falling.

I am so glad about this I cannot keep it to myself!

In you, Lord, I am completely secure!

Psalm 16

A Prayer for Times of Persecution

L ord, I have done what is right and just,
   therefore do not let me fall into the capricious clutches
of my enemies.

Please, promise me that everything will be all right.

Do not allow self-aggrandizing people to oppress me.

O Righteous God, I long for your salvation--
   when you will set me free as you have promised.

You love me, Lord. Please help me;
   give me insight into your ways.

I turn my life over to you;
   give me understanding of Your precepts
   that I may find in them your will for my life.

Lord, isn't it time for you to intervene
   against those who disobey your commandments?

I love your law--it is more precious to me than pure gold.

I despise every kind of untruth and falsehood.

Your infallible precepts are trustworthy guides
   only for those who desire an upstanding, decent life.

Psalm 119, Stanza 16

A Prayer for Times of Poverty and Deprivation

Lord, for how long will I feel as if you have forgotten me?

How long will it seem like you are far away?

How long will my worries continually agonize me?

How long will troubles go on gnawing at me day after day?

Please, Lord, God, turn to me once again and answer me.

Allow me to be happy again and to gain courage,

otherwise death will surely overcome me.

My enemy would triumph and say, "I ran him down!"

My oppressors would rejoice at my death.

But I trust in your love.

I rejoice, for you will surely rescue me.

I will praiseyou with my song

for you have been so good to me.

Psalm 13

A Prayer to Overcome Temptation

L ord, because I love you with all my heart,
  I detest when people are wishy-washy about following you,
  Only in you am I secure;
    you are my refuge, my protection.
  I put all my hope in your promises.

Away with you, evildoers!
My God commands and directs my life:
You will not hinder me from obeying him.

Lord, hold firmly onto me, according to your promise, that I may revive.
Please do not allow me to hope in vain or lose courage.
Set me on the straight and narrow path, Lord, that I may be made well.
I desire to be constantly occupied with obeying your commands.

For you will reject anyone who disowns your ordinances.
And whoever tries to fool you, harms himself.
You eliminate those who despise you;
  you toss them out like garbage.

Psalm 119, Stanza 15

O Lord, I love your precepts.

When I consider that you know and judge all my thoughts
 and deeds,

  I shudder in fear.

Psalm 119, Stanza 15

A Prayer for Violent Times

L ord, hear my prayer.
  Please be mindful of my request and answer me.
I can always rely on you because you keep your word.
Do not bring me into your court of judgment,
  for no one stands innocent before You.

The enemy pursues my soul;
  I feel as if I'm in darkness, forgotten,
  as if I'm already dead.
I don't know what to do—
  I'm paralyzed by fear.

I think back to earlier times,
  remembering all the great miracles you performed.
I keep your mighty works in my mind's eye.
I stretch out my hands to you in supplication.
Like a desert thirsting for water,
  I wait longingly for you to intervene.

Lord, answer me quickly—I've reached my limit!
If you forsake me, I will not endure.

Show me every morning that you intend good things for
  me,
  because I trust in You.
I lift up my needy soul to you.

Psalm 143

Show me which path to take;
  rescue me from my enemies.
Only in you do I find a safe refuge.

Help me to live according to your will,
  for you are everything to me, my God!
Revive me; remove the obstacles from my path
  that I may live joyfully.

Lord, I depend on your promises—please help me in my
  dire need.
If you preserve my life,
  it will bring honor and glory to your name.
Eradicate my enemies,
  destroy those who have brought me to despair.
I put my trust entirely in you,
  for you are my master.
I serve and obey you.

Psalm 143

Part Two:

Daily Scripture Study

After you draw nearer to God in prayer, open your heart and mind to his will for your life by listening to his word.

Use this section of the book to consider what God's word tells you about prayer by using the ancient practice of *lectio divina* (pronounced LEX-ee-o di-VEEN-ah), or sacred reading.

When you come to a footnote, stop, look up the scripture, and reflect on it. Ask what the text says, and also what it says to you. Then, talk to God about the text, the way you would talk to someone who listens carefully to the stirrings of your heart. And finally, consider how this text makes a difference—how it changes or transforms your life.[1] Don't hurry this journey. One scripture passage per day, considered deeply, is enough. You can use an ordinary spiral bound notebook or any kind of journal, sketchbook, or binder, to ponder the word of God and record any thoughts, impressions and decisions that come to you.

For those who want more guidance with this process, we have written and published the *Nearer to God Journal*.

---

1   Daniel J. Harrington, SJ's, four easy steps for *lectio*, as taught to James Martin, SJ and published in Martin's essay "Teach Us to Pray," in *Give Us This Day*, a guide to daily prayer by Liturgical Press, April 2016.

6) The Narrow Way

Two Paths—Two Destinations

There is one path, which leads to the kingdom of God, and it is narrow. The way to hell, however, is broad and its gate is wide. Most people will opt for the seemingly more convenient and comfortable way. But we must remember this: the door that leads to eternal life is small, and the way that leads to God is narrow. And because it is not easy, few will choose to travel the narrow way. [1]

The Wayfarer Chooses[2]

The wayfarer,
Perceiving the pathway to truth,
Was struck with astonishment.
It was thickly grown with weeds.
"Ha," he said,
"I see that none has passed here
In a long time."
Later he saw that each weed was a singular knife.
"Well," he mumbled at last,
"Doubtless there are other roads."[3]

---

1 Matthew 7: 13-14
2 Joshua 24:15
3 This is Stephen Crane's poem, *The Wayfarer,* likely written in the 1890's.

Yes, there are other roads. We must, however, be aware that every other road is false, leading to devastation and destruction.[4] Only the narrow way will guide us closer to God.

Watch for the Signs[5]

Everything we need, in order to live in a way that pleases God, has been given to us in Jesus Christ.[6] For in Jesus we come to know God,[7] who, through his power and glory, has called us to a better way of life. By calling us to him, he gives us the greatest, most valuable gift: his promise that everyone who forsakes the corrupt practices of this world will inherit a place in his eternal, heavenly kingdom.[8]

Therefore we must work to our utmost, and prove by our exemplary moral conduct that we believe what God says. If we are truly walking the narrow way, everyone will recognize that we know God. Our right relationship with God will be evident in our self-control, which can only be learned through patient endurance. And patient endurance will teach us to truly love and revere God.

Finally, if we sincerely love God, we will also love our brothers and sisters in Christ. Our love for one another will be so completely evident, that everyone will see and recognize it by our actions.

The only way to insure that our faith will not be fruitless and meaningless, is to follow the narrow way and continually make progress. Therefore, we channel all of our energy into that for which God has called and chosen us. If we keep our

---

4 Luke 13:22-28
5 Jeremiah 31:21
6 2 Peter 1:3
7 1 John 2:23
8 Matthew 19:29

priorities straight, we will not stray from the narrow path, and the door to the eternal kingdom of our Lord and Savior Jesus Christ will open for us. [9]

Clear signs that we are walking the narrow way:

• Our moral conduct is exemplary;[10]

• We exhibit self-control;[11]

• We acquire patient endurance;[12]

• We sincerely love and revere God;[13]

• Our love for God is made visible by our demonstrated love for others.[14]

• We fear[15] and worship[16] God.

• We are humble and contrite.[17]

• We do not judge or condemn anyone else.[18]

• We submit to God.[19]

• Our prayers are mediated by Jesus.[20]

• Our prayers are inspired by the Holy Spirit.[21]

---

9 2 Peter 1: 3-11
10 Proverbs 11:5-15
11 Proverbs 25:28
12 Hebrews 10:36-39
13 Deuteronomy 6:5
14 1 John 4:20
15 Ecclesiastes 12:13-14
16 Exodus 23:25
17 Psalm 51:17
18 Matthew 7:1-5
19 2nd Chronicles 30:8
20 1st Timothy 2:5
21 Romans 8:15

7) Requirements

Those who successfully finish a long hike understand that time, strength and stamina are required. And we who wish to successfully draw nearer to God must also know what is required to reach our goal.

We Must Be Inspired

To pray prophetically is to submit our hearts and minds to the will of God, in order to open our lives to the work of the Holy Spirit.[1] We begin to do this simply by believing the word of God and speaking it, in the name of Jesus Christ,[2] by the power of the Holy Spirit,[3] into our particular situations, triumphs, problems, joys and concerns.[4] While this may sound easy, it is a difficult and lifelong task, because our hearts are stubborn and are minds are willful.[5] We cannot accomplish this by our own will or motive, and no human can teach us how to submit to God. We need the Spirit of God to instruct us.[6]

1 Acts 7:51
2 Colossians 3:17
3 1 Corinthians 14:14-15
4 Philippians 4:6
5 Jeremiah 5:23
6 1 John 2:27

We Must Be Committed

As with all practices and relationships, a commitment to diligent effort leads to continual improvement and better results.[7]

We Must Be in love with God

Those who pray with prophetic power seek to please God with the entirety of their beings—their hearts, minds, souls and strength. This is what it means to love God.[8] When this love happens to us, our purpose for living becomes purely Christ-like; we desire only to do the will of God.[9] We delight in whatever God wants, and we find our utmost joy in obedience to his Word. And when we are in right relationship with God, he blesses us, protects us, shines his light into our darkness, is gracious to us, looks upon us with pleasure, and gives us peace.[10]

We Must Be Aware

Consider what happens when we don't love God, when we prefer our own will to his, when it pleases us to go our own way. Instead of inheriting blessings, we are cursed. We run headlong into trouble and danger and we get no help. Confusion and chaos surround us, and we fall into depravity, depression and despair. We lose God's grace and favor. He looks upon us with anger, and he punishes us exactly as we deserve to be punished.[11] Instead of living in peace, we live in tormented confusion.[12]

7 2 Corinthians 8:11
8 Luke 10:27
9 John 4:34
10 Numbers 6:25
11 Isaiah 13:11
12 Romans 1:18

We must accept that God does not listen to the prayers of those who reject him; but he listens to those who seek to do his will. [13]

We Must Be Right

The Apostles of Jesus Christ, nearly 2000 years ago, warned us that there will be many people who make a mockery of the faith. These people profess to believe in Jesus, but they are guided by their own ambitions and desires.[14] All their thoughts and deeds are focused on worldly success. God's spirit is not in them.[15] These people are deceitful, and they cause divisions in the body of Christ.[16]

We must not allow ourselves to be led astray from the purity and simplicity of devotion to Christ.[17] God himself has instilled faith in us, and we must protect it.[18]

This faith is the foundation of true life. Whenever we pray, we must allow ourselves to be inspired by the power of the Holy Spirit. This will insure that our prayers will be right, and we will always remain wholly in love with God,[19] while we wait patiently for the coming of God's kingdom, when our Lord Jesus, the Messiah, will triumphantly lead us into eternal life.[20]

---

13 John 9:31
14 Jude 1:4
15 James 4:4
16 Romans 16:17
17 2 Corinthians 11:3
18 Jude 1:3
19 Revelation 2:4
20 Jude 1:18-21

8) Burdens and Provisions

Only a fool would attempt to hike the Appalachian Trail without a backpack to carry appropriate food, shelter and clothing. Long-distance trekkers understand that provisioning also includes choosing to *not* carry along heavy canned goods, perishable food, mattresses, tables, chairs, dishes, televisions sets, and a closet full of clothes and shoes.

In the same way, we who choose to walk the narrow way must divest ourselves of the weight of any burden, which makes it difficult for us to make progress.

After we have relinquished all that we should not carry, we must provision ourselves with spiritual strengths, which empower us to journey nearer to God.

The Bible has a metaphoric name for the burdens that hinder us: they are called *lusts of the flesh.* The strengths that empower us are called *fruits of the Spirit.*[1]

Particular *lusts* (hindrances) and *fruits* (empowerments) are listed on the next two pages.

---

1 Galatians 5:16-26

Lusts are Burdens

Divesting ourselves of burdens, we renounce everything that opposes the will of God for our lives:

- Adultery[2]
- Fornication[3]
- Impurity[4]
- Lewdness[5]
- Idolatry[6]
- Sorcery / Witchcraft[7]
- Hatred[8]
- Contentiousness[9]
- Jealousy[10]
- Outbursts of Wrath[11]
- Self-aggrandizing Ambitions[12]
- Dissensions and Heresies[13]
- Envy[14]
- Violence and Murder[15]
- Drunkeness[16] and Carousing[17]

---

2 Exodus 20:14
3 1st Corinthians 6:18-20
4 Matthew 5:8
5 Ephesians 5:4
6 Romans 1:22-23
7 Deuteronomy 18:9-12
8 1st John 3:15
9 Proverbs 17:19
10 James 3:16
11 Psalm 37:8
12 Matthew 23:12
13 1st Corinthians 1:10
14 Proverbs 23:17
15 Exodus 20:13
16 Ephesians 5:18
17 Romans 13:13

Fruits are Provisions

For spiritual nourishment, we allow the Holy Spirit to empower us to develop attitudes which help us carry out the will of God:

- Love[18]
- Joy[19]
- Peace[20]
- Patient Endurance[21]
- Kindness[22]
- Goodness[23]
- Faithfulness[24]
- Gentleness[25]
- Self-control[26]

As we draw ever closer to God, we become empowered by the Holy Spirit to relinquish selfish desires and adopt spiritual habits, so that our lives become increasingly authentically *good*.[27]

We remind ourselves that authentic goodness is always reflective of the nature and character of God, because only God is good.[28]

---

18 Luke 6:32
19 Philemon 1:7
20 2nd Corinthians 13:11
21 Hebrews 10:36
22 Ephesians 4:32
23 James 3:13
24 Luke 12:42-44
25 Proverbs 15:1
26 1st Peter 4:7
27 Galations 6:25-26
28 Mark 10:18

9) Transformations

The Appalachian Trail, from Springer Mountain in Georgia to Mount Katahdin in Maine, is over two-thousand miles long. It goes on and on. It's grueling, and yet people *choose* to hike the AT. Their stories inspire thousands more, every year, to put on their boots and carry their packs. People willingly undertake this hardship because it is well-known that long and difficult journeys lead to transformation.

Have you ever noticed the similarity between the words *trail* and *trial*? Drawing nearer to God so our prayers will be effective is a long and difficult journey. It is also the way we accomplish transformations.

Prophetically Powerful Prayer overcomes evil with goodness

Prophetically powerful prayer moves mountains.[1] Self-centered desires and egotistical motives; immorality; impurity; self-indulgence; idolatry; vain superstition and trust in supernatural powers; hostilities; contentious quarrelsomeness; erratic fits of jealousy; discord and dissension; schisms and envy; addiction; extravagant waste and destruction of resources; everything in opposition to the sovereign will of God is dismantled and destroyed by prophetically powerful prayer.[2]

When we are confronted by any of these mountainous forces, in ourselves or in others, we are called to pray.

---

1 Matthew 21:21
2 Galatians 5:19-21

Prophetically powerful prayer facilitates the work of the Holy Spirit so that our love, joy, peace, patience, gentleness, cheerfulness, kindness, faithfulness, discretion and self-control may increase.[3] Whenever these virtuous fruits of the Spirit are lacking or weak in ourselves or in others, we are called to pray.

Prophetically Powerful Prayer changes the One Who Prays

Blessed are those who have a need, who turn to God believing they are his beloved children.[4]

Blessed are those who recognize their powerlessness; who realize they are weak and incapable of fixing their problems; who realzie they are utterly helpless:

• God will abide with them.

Blessed are those who experience betrayal, violence and injustice:

• God will comfort them.

Blessed are those who regret the harm they have done to others and to God's creation; whose own wrongdoing causes guilt to sear their consciences and grief to fill their souls:

• God will forgive them.

Blessed are those who relinquish their own plans, dreams and desires, who submit their lives to God in the knowledge that his precepts and pronouncements are just, right and true:

• they are God's children, inheriting all the spiritual treasures of his kingdom.

---

3 Galatians 5:22
4 This section is our contemporary amplified translation of the Beattitudes, from Matthew 5:3-12

Blessed are those who yearn for justice and righteousness; who are appalled by every evil motive and every evil deed; who ardently long for authentic goodness:

- they will be drawn ever closer to the holiness of God.

Blessed are those who enter into God's holiness and thereby learn compassion; for whom the suffering of others causes pain; who are compelled to condemn, alleviate and heal the tragic results of humanity's envy, greed, hatred and revenge:

- they will know and experience God's amazing loving-kindness.

Blessed are those whose motives for helping others remains untainted by a lust for personal power and recognition; who relinquish their desire to feel important; who understand that only God can melt the heart of a bitter, angry or indifferent person; whose deepest desire is to daily do the will of God with sincere humility:

- they will be drawn ever closer to God.

Blessed are those who make it their daily practice to: recognize their powerlessness; grieve their sins and ask God's forgiveness; suffer injustice and forgive the perpetrators; submit their lives to God; seek justice; demonstrate compassion to everyone including the undeserving; and cast off every self-aggrandizing thought and motivation:

- they will behold God and know his unsurpassed peace.

Blessed are those so filled with the knowledge of God's peace that they effortlessly carry peace into their dealings and conversations with everyone; who so emanate God's peace that their presence stifles arguments and extinguishes violent intentions:

- they will be recognized as the children of God.

Blessed are those whose lives resemble the prophets of old, who, because they do the will of God, are therefore insulted, persecuted, slandered and defamed:

> • assuredly the kingdom of God is within them, and their eternal heavenly reward will be great.

They will rejoice exceedlingly, for they are abundantly blessed.

10) Our Destination

You are great, O Lord,
   and greatly to be praised…

for you have made us for yourself,[1]
and our heart is restless
until it rests in you.[2]

The Confessions of Saint Augustine,
Book One: God and the Soul

To *rest* in God, we must *trust* God.

To *trust* God, we must *know* God.

To *know* God, we must *understand* and *believe* what God
reveals to us about Himself.

The study of God's revelation, of His Word, is a lifelong
journey. As we journey nearer to God, we remind ourselves
where we are going and what we aspire to be, by considering
the character of the Creator / Redeemer / Sanctifier, who calls
us to ever draw nearer to God.

---

1   Psalm 100:3
2   Psalm 139

God Is

Eternal--Isaiah 57:15

Feared–Exodus 1:15-21

Good–Psalm 100:5

Gracious–1ˢᵗ Peter 5:10

Holy–1ˢᵗ Peter 1:16

Infinite–Psalm 147:5

Jealous–Deuteronomy 4:24

Just–2ⁿᵈ Thessalonians 1:6

All-Knowing–Hebrews 4:13

Love–1ˢᵗ John 4:8

Merciful–Ephesians 2:4

All-Powerful–Psalm 62:11

Sovereign–1ˢᵗ Chronicles 29:11-12

Unchanging–Matthew 24:39

All-Wise–Romans 16:27

Onward

> "The seduction of embarking on a spiritual life is that people can be fooled into believing that wanting it is doing it. They begin to believe that by traveling they have arrived."[1]

In order to continue onward in the spiritual life, we recommend the following:

- Develop the habit of listening for the still, small voice of God through the ancient practice of sacred reading. One way to start is to slowly, carefully, re-read this book, covering just one footnote per day. Look up the footnote text in your Bible, and engage with it. We have published the *Nearer to God Journal,* as a useful tool for this process.

- Read *The Rule of Benedict: A Spirituality for the 21st Century* by Joan Chittister, OSB. This practical guide based on early-church wisdom takes us deeper into conversion, draws us ever nearer to God, and thereby releases the power of God's love to transform our relationships and our world.

- To learn to practice the radical kindness of Jesus in all your relationships, read *Radical Hospitality* by Lonnie Collins Pratt with Father Daniel Homan, OSB © 2011.

---

1   *The Rule of Benedict: A Spirituality for the 21st Century.* by Joan Chittister, OSB. © 2010. Used with permission of The Crossroad Publishing Company, www.crossroadpublishing.com.

Our prayer for you is that you will be inspired to draw ever nearer to God, and be strengthened with the necessary perseverence to continue on that quest.

We hope you continue to daily worship God in prayer, read the word of God and ponder it, in order to *know* God, *trust* God, and *return* to God...[1]

...that you may ever and always *rest* in God.

---

1 James 4:10

Index of Psalms

with King James Version first lines

About the Authors

Ken and Tracy Lee Karner were married in 1993, at which time they committed their lives and their marriage to sharing the love of Jesus the Messiah with each other, and with everyone they encounter. Despite their many failings, God's saving power continues to be a beacon of hope and comfort to them, as they navigate life's joys and sorrows, purposefully seeking to draw ever nearer to God.

To learn more, visit Tracy's website:

TracyLeeKarner.com